HEARTS STRANGELY WARMED

Reflections on Biblical Passages Relevant to Social Work

Edited by Lawrence E. Ressler

Preface

Following are some scriptures which Christian social workers and pastors supportive of social work have found meaningful in their own lives. Many but not all of them were written by students or pastors associated with the Carver School of Church Social Work, a MSW program of The Southern Baptist Theological Center.

Most of the essays were written between 1987 and 1992 at the invitation of Dr. Anne Davis, then dean of the Carver School. A committee of three persons in the fall of 1993 read the nearly 100 essays which had been written and rated them according to the writing, theology, and application to social work. The following essays were selected to be included in this collection. A few additional essays from persons not related to the Carver School were added.

With the exception of the I Corinthians 13 passage which uses the Revised Standard Version, the scriptures are quoted from the New International Version. For consistency and simplicity, passages have been quoted as translated including the use of the masculine variations of words that more recently use neutral terms.

These essays are presented to bring encouragement to you as you strive to bring health, wholeness, reconciliation to those in need. May they give you strength and insight to do the good works that are in you.

Lawrence E. Ressler

Table of Contents

Genesis 6:5-8

The Lord saw how great man's wickedness on the earth had become, and that every inclination of the thoughts of his heart was only evil all the time. The Lord was grieved that he had made man on the earth, and his heart was filled with pain. So the Lord said, "I will wipe mankind whom I have created, from the face of the earth - men and animals, and creatures that move along the ground, and birds of the air - for I am grieved that I have made them." But Noah found favor in the eyes of the Lord.

This passage provides the bedrock on which Christian social work is founded. We find in these verses the essence of history, a glimpse of the character of God, and a framework for our helping.

The world, in this account, is in a mess and God is in pain. The creation which had delighted God is now in turmoil. The gap between the beauty of creation and ugliness of evil is so great, we find God nearly overwhelmed with grief, so much so that he is sorry he made mankind, so much pain he thinks of destroying it all.

Social workers know the feeling. We have seen the gift of childhood crushed by sexual or physical abuse. We have watched as the beauty of family life was destroyed by a parent a with alcoholism. We have seen enjoyment of life die as the harsh realities of poverty took over. We have ached as we have watched the marvelous human body wither away under the ravages of AIDS. We have felt the anguish of those who have been discriminated against because of race or ethnicity. We know, like God, something is very wrong and it hurts to the core of our being. We have felt the pain so deeply that we, like God, wonder if life is worth it. We, like God, know this is not the way things are supposed to be.

But God did not destroy his creation. He began a process of reconciliation - taking individuals one at a time, groups one at a time and remaking them. First there was Noah, then Abraham, Issaac, Jacob - on and on throughout history. God cared enough to not give up on his creation. He cared enough to send his son, God incarnate, to live among us, suffer for and with us, that we might live again.

This passage can, oddly enough, give us hope and inspiration. As friends of God, we are here to carry on his work. In spite of the pain around us, we, like God, care enough about the painful situations people are in to hang in there. We are called, as Paul says in II Corinthians, to be ministers of reconciliation. We take the child with a shattered soul and try to find healing. We immerse ourselves in the painful world of a family in distress and work for peace. Rather than run from a world of injustice, we struggle for justice.

As we feel the pain of broken lives and see the evils of twisted culture, we can move beyond despair and offer hope.

Lawrence Ressler

II
Genesis 44:34

How can I go back to my father if the boy is not with me?
No! Do not let me see the misery that would come upon my
father.

Judah, spokesperson for the tribe of Jacob had the responsibility of
returning Benjamin safely to his father in Canaan. Upon Joseph's request, they had taken their youngest brother to Egypt to buy food for
their families. In a vengeful moment, Joseph hid the silver cup in
Benjamin's sack and demanded that Benjamin become his slave. Even
though the brothers were innocent of the crime, it appeared that Judah
would not be able to follow through with his promise.

I cannot help but think about the horrible things that Judah and his
brothers had done to Joseph years before. Although Judah appeared to
have changed his non-caring attitude toward his father's favorite son,
his past actions rendered very serious consequences. His father would
probably disown him and he would have to live with the guilt and
shame for the rest of his life.

As social workers we have been called to care for people when they
are hurting and to show them God's love. Our responsibility goes beyond caring for the spiritual needs of the person to include their physical, emotional, and social needs. But sometimes our ability to respond
to people is hampered by our past actions or inactions. Although
Judah's intentions were good, his past actions limited his ability to act
responsibly.

A modern-day example of this can be seen in the increased use of
drugs and alcohol among teenagers. If people do not act responsibly by
teaching teens to cope with stresses of adolescence and by teaching
families to deal more effectively with their children, the world may end
up being led by drug and alcohol addicts. Then it will be too late for us
to act responsibly. The opportunity and ability to act responsibly will be
gone.

Sarah Willoughby

3

III
Deuteronomy 2:1-3

Then we turned back and set out toward the desert along the route to the Red Sea, as the Lord had directed me. For a long time we made our way around the hill country of Seir. Then the Lord said to me, "You have made your way around this hill country long enough: now turn north."

In *All God's Children Need Traveling Shoes*, Maya Angelou tells of her pilgrimage to Africa. She was thirty-three years old, adventuresome and determined. She muses:

> We had come home, and if home was not what we had expected, never mind, our need for belonging allowed us to ignore the obvious and to create real places... befitting our imagination. We didn't question if we would be useful. Our people for over three hundred years had been so useful, a bloody war had been fought and lost, rather than have our usefulness brought to an end. Since we were descendants of African slaves torn from the land, we reasoned we wouldn't be so arrogant as to take anything for granted. We would work and produce, then snuggle down into Africa as a baby nuzzles in a mother's arms.

Like Angelou, the Israelites were traveling to a place familiar and yet unknown. Generations earlier, famine removed them from their homeland; Egyptian task-masters made slaves of them. They eventually escaped and began the homeward journey which was punctuated by thirty-eight years of circling Kadesh and the neighboring wilderness. In Deuteronomy 2, we learn that God gave traveling orders to his wandering people. The following years were filled with struggles to claim a land and make it a home.

What about us? As did Angelou and the Israelites, we may discover that our need for belonging pushes us haltingly toward some goal. We may be uncertain of our destination. Or we may know it all too well and choose to circle around for many days, shrinking from the battles to be faced in claiming the land or the sheepskin. God calls us to continue on the way. As social workers, the goal may demand that we tenaciously "ignore the obvious to create real places... befitting our imagination." We may know God's promise of guidance until we reach home.

In gratitude to the One who leads us, we humbly bow our heads.

Janet E. Cash

Deuteronomy 6:4-9

Hear , O Israel: The Lord our God, the Lord is one. Love the Lord your God with all your heart and with all your soul and with all your strength. These commandments that I give you today are to be upon your hearts. Impress them on your children. Talk about them when you sit at home and when you walk along the road, when you lie down and when you get up. Tie them as symbols on your hands and bind them on your foreheads. Write them on the doorframes of your houses and on your gates.

This great commandment calls us to love God with all that we are and with all that we do. I sometimes feel that loving God is just one more thing that I must or should be doing. This can become one more demand, one more stress, and one more way for me to blame myself for not being a "good enough Christian." Somewhere I have learned to separate God into a category labelled "out there." God can become for me, if I am not careful, this mysterious being who is not a real part of my daily living, but one whom I worship and pray to alone in my room or in a sanctuary on Sunday morning.   While personal meditation, prayer, and corporate worship are some of the ways we love God, I believe this passage encourages us to integrate God into our whole lives, not just a part of them. Loving God is not something we set aside to do. Loving God is the way we live and the people we love. To separate our religious life into a "spiritual dimension" which does not incorporate our concrete social relationships is to limit the ways we love God.

This passage tells us to love God "with all our heart, and with all our soul and with all our might" through the activities and relationships of our daily life. Lord, help us to love you in all that we do and say. Make this our continuing prayer.

Jeanine Siler Jones

II Kings 19:29-30

This will be the sign for you, O Hezekiah: this year you will eat what grows by itself, and the second year what springs from that. But in the third year sow and reap, plant vineyards and eat their fruit. Once more a remnant of the house of Judah will take root below and bear fruit above.

There is much deliverance in the Old Testament. As one proceeds to investigate these historic and victorious happenings, it becomes apparent that prayer is an everpresent resource of strength for the discouraged and struggling believer.

In II Kings 19, Hezekiah's faith in God is strengthened by the fulfillment of a prayer. An enemy invasion prevents the people of Judah from planting the needed seasonal crops. The following year is to be the traditional seasonal sabbatical year. The people of Judah are frightened that there will not be sufficient crops to provide for the people during the two lost planting seasons. Hezekiah prays for plentiful crops. He is assured by God that there will be sufficient crops to meet the people's need.

Faith is finding confidence and trust in God. Prayer is the means of expressing that faith. It is well when our troubles drive us to our knees because it reminds us of who we are and who God is. "Root downward and bear fruit upward."

As we engage in our helping, let us strive to root in God; believing in the assurance of God's presence. And just as a plant that is rooted in good soil bears fruit, so also will we bear fruit; a life filled with confidence to meet the outward struggles of our work as well as the inward foes.

Jane Barker

II Chronicles 7:14

If my people, who are called by my name, will humble themselves and pray and seek my face and turn from their wicked ways, then will I hear from heaven and will forgive their sin and will heal their land.

War in the middle-east, oil spills, murder, nuclear waste dumps, robbery, ozone alert... and the list goes on. Words from the modern-day newscaster are a daily reminder of the world in which we live and of the condition of those with whom we meet. We are faced with the question, "What are we to do and how can we make a difference in a world full of such deeds and negative consequences?"

Emerging in the midst of this question is an answer so simple but also equally true. Seek the heart of a loving God. A heart which calls us into possession as "my people" and a heart which gives us a call of adoption by "my name." As we take on the heart of God in prayer and humility of spirit, salvation can be accomplished for ourselves and for those whom God would send to us to teach. Prayer places us at God's disposal in child-like dependence, completely aware of our sins and imperfections. Indeed as we understand the heart of God we receive forgiveness and healing as individuals.

Yet it is not enough to only find God's heart for ourselves. We must be willing to get off our knees and move into action to accomplish with our minds and bodies the mission God would have us accomplish. We must find in our own healing and in our own restoration to God's heart the motivation to "heal the land." The land is an open wound and the suffering, destruction, waste and apathy towards God is a source of grief not only to those of us who care about our world but to the heart of God who would desire to truly "heal the land."

Marilynn Jo Ford

Job 29:1-6

Job continued his discourse: "How I long for the months gone by, for the days when God watched over me, when his lamp shone upon my head and by his light I walked through darkness! Oh, for the days when I was in my prime, when God's intimate friendship blessed my house, when the Almighty was still with me and my children were around me, when my path was drenched with cream and the rock poured out for me streams of olive oil."

Every generation looks back to their "good old days." Here, Job recalls the blessings and ease of his past. Those days seem now to have been full of the presence and guidance of the almighty God. Life was simple. Problems were nowhere to be seen. The problems that were nowhere to be seen were, however, lurking in the shadows, waiting. Now Job finds himself in the midst of problems, and with the entrance of problems comes the seeming exit of God.

And thus I find myself speaking the words of Job, longing for "the good old days." I am bombarded with problems of life at the seminary: papers to write, books to read, tests to take. I wrestle with the problems of living: bills to pay, dirty dishes to wash, cars that won't run. I struggle with myself, a minister in the making; personal time with God, witnessing to others, caring for the marginal.

Suddenly, in the midst of it all, a voice from deep within calls out, "Where are the good old days?" Why can't I be sitting beside my daddy on Sunday morning, my hand tucked in his crossed arms, unaware of the decisions and responsibilities that race through his mind as he listens to the preacher?" What are the pictures of your "good old days?"

However, the story does not end here with a plea for the comforts of days gone by. Job stood fast amidst suffering. He continued to believe amidst confusion, and God was there all along. God knew of all the struggles Job had inside and out. We must stand firm also. God is right there, listening.

Lyle Greene

Job 42:5-6

My ears had heard of you but now my eyes have seen you.
Therefore, I despise myself and repent in dust and ashes.

What a sad character is Job! What low self esteem! What kind of morbid religion would cause him to despise himself so? Job's words are strange to many of us. We have long since renounced the kind of theology that allowed Isaac Watts to ask, "Would he devote that sacred head, for such a worm as I?" We prefer to ascribe to the gospel messages of love, affirmation, and positive self imaging. Yet something worthy of our attention is present in Job's strange words.

The ancients believed that if one were to see the face of God, one would surely die. Remember Moses? In spite of his pleas to see God face to face, he was allowed only to see God's back. For the ancients it was an awesome and moving experience to find oneself in the presence of God. To encounter God was to see the world and oneself in a whole new light. Isaiah, upon encountering God in the temple, was moved to confess and commit his life in a whole new direction.

A look at God causes us to look at ourselves anew. In the encounter with God death does occur. In the presence of God, we can no longer hold on to our self delusions. We die to the illusions we have of our righteousness, integrity, and spirituality. We die to the false images of the selves upon which we have built our lives.

Painful? Yes. To see oneself as one really is, stripped of all pretense, can throw life into turmoil. But it can also give God the opportunity to transform our existence by God's grace.

Guilt, confession, and repentance, are not signs of an unhealthy religious experience. They can open the door to God's grace.

Jim Holladay

Psalm 27:1

The Lord is my light and my salvation—whom shall I fear? The Lord is the stronghold of my life—of whom shall I be afraid?

The psalmist had a good memory. Because of that memory he could state this confession of faith with confidence. What did the psalmist have faith in? First, he had faith in a Lord that was his light. This light had seen him through many anxious, troubled, and dangerous times. Second, the psalmist had faith in a Lord who was his salvation. He had seen his Lord deliver him when it seemed impossible. Third, the psalmist had faith in a Lord who was his strength. He had realized that the Lord was the one who sustained his life.

The psalmist asked two questions in response to these memories. They were: "Whom shall I fear?" and "Of whom shall I be afraid?" The psalmist refused to be afraid of what people could do to him. For he had seen the Lord in his past provide light in darkness, deliverance in times of trouble, and strength in times of weakness.

Even in the midst of all that we do as social workers, we need to begin to build memories of how the Lord has met our needs. In the future we will be able to look back and remember the Lord in whom we have faith.

Let us learn through our own experiences and memories, that we have nothing to fear with the Lord.

Frank Martin

X
Psalm 137:1-6

By the rivers of Babylon, there we sat down and wept, when we remembered Zion. On the willows there we hung up our lyres. For there our captors required of us songs, and our tormentors, mirth, saying "Sing us one of the songs of Zion!" How shall we sing the Lord's song in a foreign land? If I forget you, O Jerusalem, let my right hand wither! Let my tongue cleave to the roof of my mouth. If I do not remember you, if I do not set Jerusalem above my highest joy!

This is a communal lament sung by the exiled Israelites as they mourned the loss of their homes, their temples, and their loved ones. As the waters flowed with life before them, so their tears flowed with death from them. Around them voices mocked their pain and their God while images of their grief haunted them from within.

As social workers in North America, most of us have not personally experienced violent displacement. For us, this lament can only be experienced vicariously as we seek to imagine the pain of these Israelites and those within our own contemporary world who are displaced from their homes.

As a community, those stories which we tell about ourselves help define who we are and how others perceive us. As a Christian community, the communal lament of Psalm 137 is part of our history and our legacy. Through the telling of this story we remind ourselves that our ancestors suffered persecution and exile for their faith. Because of this event, and events like it, our faith has been indelibly marked by suffering; suffering that found its ultimate expression in the suffering of Jesus.

Working with those who have experienced, and are experiencing, the suffering of displacement, we can draw upon this lament as a touch-point for communication. We may not know their pain, but we do acknowledge that our religious experience is derived from such pain as theirs. We can also hold out the hope that as our ancestors ultimately found that God was still with them in Babylon, so too is God with those who have experienced such violence today.

John Hippe

Proverbs 3:5-6

Trust in the Lord with all your heart and lean not on your own understanding; in all your ways acknowledge him, and he will make your paths straight.

We are invited, in this passage, to exercise a kind of trust which transcends the most humiliating human conditions. This kind of trust is exemplified by Jeremiah while in captivity. Isolated from his people and from his task, the prophet is able to keep his vision. From the filthy dungeon where he was held, God's servant dares to speak of a successful outcome; and while practically facing death, he speaks of life. Human beings experience life situations that produce a sense of alienation and imprisonment; life's dead-ends. We need to be reminded: "Trust in the Lord."

Probably writing in a more relaxed atmosphere than Jeremiah, the Psalmist pictures the trusting child of God as an imperturbable mountain (Psalm 125:1). Down by the hillside is the village where each home represents a private world complete with visions, ambitions, wishes, problems and desires; people and circumstances move against each other as if in an eternal dance. The mountain remains. Seasons come and go; the mountain quietly dresses in white during winter and joyfully in green during spring. Fall gives her a multicolored outfit and summer offers her countless visitors. It is as if the circumstances were made to beautify the mountain. Each season represents new life emerging from decay. Could we feel like a mountain amid uncontrollable circumstances?

A popular song during the 80's exhorted humans to lean on a friend because sooner or later the supportive friend might need support. "Lean on me," the song went, "cause it won't be long, when I'll need a friend to help me carry on." Expected reciprocation among humans is a common phenomenon. This is not the case in God's grace. God's love overflows unconditionally upon the just and the unjust. Even when our sin was great, God's grace was greater.

Parallel to these feelings of abandonment there is another invitation which involves more than just feelings. It involves thought processes: Acknowledge God. Perhaps the easiest way to understand our acknowledgment of God, would be to remember instances where we attempted to be useful to someone else. We wanted to be part of the solution and yet received only a patronizing pat-on-the-back. The real message was: "Yes, yes I know that you care, but I don't feel that you're the one I need right now." During stressful times, an individual could easily become a narcissistic narrow-minded seeker of solutions.

Acknowledging someone requires focused attention on the object of our acknowledgment. Do we acknowledge God or do we just say a little patronizing prayer? Do we feel and think what, why, when, and how we pray to God?

Donoso Escobar

Isaiah 30:15-16

This is what the Soverign Lord, the Holy One of Israel, says: " In repentance and rest is your salvation, in quietness and trust is your strength, but you would have none of it. You said, 'No, we will flee on horses.' Therefore you will flee! You said, 'We will ride off on swift horses.' Therefore your pursuers will be swift!"

Social work — the very title conjures up visions of harried people who with tender hearts are trying to accomplish more than is possible with too few resources. If you are like me, it is easy to get caught up in all the busyness and forget the words, "rest" and "quietness." The words, "speed" and "pressure" begin to characterize my life.

As I try to accomplish all that I have set before me, I tend to forget the importance of returning to God. As Page Kelly says in the Broadman Bible Commentary, true security and stability come from "calmly trusting in his promised help and in resting from feverish efforts to secure our own safety." We must continuously struggle with trusting in God rather than ourselves in the complex situations we face.

Ramona Conrad

XIII
Isaiah 37:31-32

Once more a remnant of the house of Judah will take root below and bear fruit above. For out of Jerusalem will come a remnant, and out of Mount Zion a band of survivors.

In this passage, Hezekiah and his people were being harassed by the Assyrian King Sennacherib, both orally and through a letter. He tried to convince Hezekiah to surrender Jerusalem to the Assyrians since God had not come to the aid of all those other cities that had already been conquered. Yet Hezekiah went to God and prayed for deliverance.

How many of us, in the midst of our daily battles, are willing to do as Hezekiah did? So often in the midst of our "down" times, we are blinded by our situation in such a way, that we seem to forget that God has promised to deliver us. When is it that we remember the "down" times the most? If not for those "down" times in which we become so vulnerable and dependent, it would be difficult to appreciate those other times of growing and becoming. . .those times in which we see God's faithfulness, mercy, and deliverance.

Many times during my journey, the Lord has brought to mind a hymn of deliverance—"Great Is Thy Faithfulness," especially the words "...thou changest not, thy compassions they fail not, as thou has been thou forever wilt be... pardon for sin and a peace that endureth, thine own dear presence to cheer and to guide; strength for today and bright hope for tomorrow. . .morning by morning new mercies I see; all I have needed thy hand hath provided, great is thy faithfulness, Lord unto me!"

In the same way in which God delivered Jerusalem to safety, God delivers us into wholeness and the privilege of serving all those others, who, like us, are looking for deliverance. Let us stop long enough in our journey to consider all the goodness and faithfulness of the God in whose promises we can depend.

Sari Laucirica

Isaiah 41:1-2

Be silent before me, you islands! Let the nations renew their strength! Let them come forward and speak: let us meet together at the place of judgment. Who has stirred up one from the east, calling him in righteousness to his service? He hands nations over to him and subdues kings before him. He turns them to dust with his sword, to windblown chaff with his bow.

These poetic words most likely come from an unnamed prophet of the exile who, in the midst of severe oppression, penned this ode of consolation on pages of persecution and tenderly presented encouragement to a people who had long been banished from their home and family and separated from the good life they once knew.

Although his message does not attack the critical issues of their misfortune, these melodic words do break forth like the song of the first bird of spring after a winter storm. They shine with the brilliance of a rainbow or the dawning of a new day. It is the "Good News" of comfort to awaken the hearts of the people with the assurance that God has not forgotten them.

His message is not that of Elijah, who called down fire from Heaven upon the corrupted system, nor was his mission that of Amos, whose fiery finger and vindictive attacked the rich, the "fat cows" who victimized the poor, robbing them of their homes, their money, and their pride.

No, this emissary of comfort came bringing a healing word to the captives, to bind up the wounded spirits of the persecuted, those crushed under the heels of tyrants, those frightened by bullies, those oppressed by slave drivers. Very delicately, God instructed his minister to comfort his people. He is to "Speak to the heart of" the people.

The message is short and to the point. Israel's iniquity is pardoned, her debts shall be forgiven her. The new day dawning brings a fresh start with the forgiveness of sin. Not only has she suffered for her own sins, but she has also suffered for the sins of others, thus receiving "Double for all her sins." Now the curse is lifted. The doors of the homeland are slowly opening and, for the hungry people, there is a land flowing with milk and honey just over the horizon.

The minister of comfort must not let the tragedy of existing conditions cloud the view of the vision. The "crier of Good News" must keep the gateway to the homeland ever before them. The long journey home will not be easy, "But they that wait upon the Lord shall renew their strength. They shall mount up with wings like eagles; they shall run and not be weary; they shall walk and faint not."

Barney Ferguson

Jeremiah 29:12-13

Then you will call upon me and come and pray to me, and
I will listen to you. You will find me when you seek me with
all your heart.

These verses describe an amazing attribute of our God. The God of
Israel and the parent of our Lord Jesus is a God that can be found. God
is not some nebulous universal force but is a personal, intimate, touch-
able being strangely acquainted with the pain of daily human existence.

The passage is found in the midst of a letter Jeremiah has written to
those carried into exile from Jerusalem to Babylon. In his letter, Jeremiah
urges the exiles to settle down and accept God's punishment by build-
ing houses, raising families, etc. Devout Jews in exile would have been
appalled by this decree and would have cried, "But we cannot seek God
in Babylon because the temple is in Jerusalem!" The Lord through
Jeremiah responds to this concern in our passage by saying, "Call me
within an obedient heart and I will listen to you. Your heart will be my
temple and as you seek me in obedience, you will find me within you."
Paul, in 1 Corinthians 3:16, shares with Christians, "Don't you know that
you yourselves are God's temple and God's Spirit lives within you?"

The God of our Lord Jesus invites you to reach out. So often our attention as social workers is drawn to the storms of life and just as the
disciples in Matthew 8:23-27, we forget that Jesus is in the boat. Jesus,
the Lord of the storm, has made a home of our hearts! He understands
the pain of disappointment, loneliness, depression, poverty, and grief
because he has experienced all that is human. Call on the Lord Jesus
where you are and He will listen.

John Hamric

Jeremiah 31:3

The Lord appeared to us in the past, saying: "I have loved you with an everlasting love; I have drawn you with loving-kindness."

In times of darkness and desolation, when God seems absent, the bright ray of God's unchanging grace shines through the living word of the prophet. These are words of hope which were addressed to the people of Israel in exile, the people of God under judgement. The words are comforting to those who have doubted the loving kindness and power of the Lord. Following this affirmation of God's love, is an assurance that God's faithfulness to the chosen covenant people also endures.

In the New Testament, the radiance of God's manifest love and grace is revealed in Christ Jesus. The light of Christ shines on, and the darkness can never master it. The love of God in Christ remains sure even when human fallenness reaches its worst. The gospel truth of the unbounded love of God gives us peace through the assurance of divine pardon and of God's transforming and empowering presence in our lives.

But the gospel of God's infinite love also disturbs our ease. Since divine love is everlasting, without limits, without considerations, without beginning or ending, and daringly inclusive, we can never be fully content in this life. How can we be unconcerned when persons face the darkness and desolation of suffering, deprivation and alienation in the world? The enduring love of the Lord, made known supremely in Christ crucified and risen, not only grants to God's people daily blessings, but offers to all God's humankind grace upon grace. Those who find themselves overcome by the love of God in Christ will, if they open themselves wholly to it, also find themselves constrained to become agents of that love. So we find ourselves drawn and driven to be instruments of God's grace-filled peace.

Paul Harris

Jeremiah 31:33-34

"This is the covenant I will make with the house of Israel after that time," declares the Lord. "I will put my law in their minds and write it on their hearts. I will be their God, and they will be my people."

He lives on the streets. Cold in the winter, he refuses to go to the mission house because "they" might hurt him. Hot in the summer, sweaty, smelly, he comes often for clean clothing. Communication with him is impossible. He either changes the subject or simply walks away not to be seen again for two or three weeks. He is a person living in the shadows of the world. You care about him and instinctively want to reach into his world. He simply walks away. You curse the system that consigns such an obviously sick man to roam the streets. You lament your own inability to be an agent of change for this man. You give up. He comes again, you try again. He walks away. You give up. Discouragement and frustration are your constant companions. This one man becomes a living parable of hopelessness. Why try?

Jeremiah, confronter of institutionalized evil, speaker to a people who would not listen, helper to those who would not be helped, has a word for us. Jeremiah, who walked with the twin companions of discouragement and frustration, knew an answer to the 'why try' question. Embodied in the revelation of a 'new covenant' he discovered a tomorrow dependent upon God's redemption not man's self-destruction. "This is the covenant," is a sign pointing to a living hope for all of us. The God of all hope is with him in the streets and with you. Because you know this truth you become a living parable hope for him. He comes back.

Jack Oliver

Amos 8:4-10

Hear this, you who trample the needy and do away with the poor of the land, saying, "When will the New Moon be over that we may sell grain, and the Sabbath be ended that we may market wheat?"— skimping the measure, boosting the price and cheating with dishonest scales, buying the poor with silver and the needy for a pair of sandals, selling even the sweepings with the wheat. The Lord has sworn by the Pride of Jacob; "I will never forget anything they have done." "Will not the land tremble for this, and all who live in it mourn? The whole land will rise like the Nile; it will be stirred up and then sink like the river of Egypt." "In that day," declares the Sovereign Lord, "I will make the sun go down at noon and darken the earth in broad daylight. I will turn your religious feasts into mourning and all your singing into weeping. I will make all of you wear sackcloth and shave your heads. I will make that time like mourning for an only son and the end of it like a bitter day."

Amos knew that religion does not always produce a concern for justice or compassion. The prophet lived in paradoxical times. Religion flourished. The economy prospered. Yet, the needy were being ground down and the poor overpowered.

The economic situation of Amos' day looks hauntingly like our own. A growing upper class with a developing urban economy created a situation where many farmers were being forced off their land. In order to survive and care for their families, these persons found it necessary to move to the urban areas in order to find work. They, along with the poor already present in the cities and towns, became more and more dependent on a market controlled by a small, wealthy, and powerful upper class.

No doubt those who were shaping the economy of the day saw themselves as wise and prudent business people. The passage even indicates they perceived themselves to be devoutly religious. God, however, saw the situation differently. God saw more than people who were developing the economy of the nation, thereby enhancing its prosperity. God saw people who were becoming wealthy at the expense of others. Through the prophet God denounces their greed and faithlessness. Unless something changed, bitter times were ahead.

James Mays, in his commentary on Amos, indicates that this passage illustrates "... the failure of faith which accompanies the success of religion..." The Apostle James affirmed that faith fails when it does not produce compassion and a desire for justice in the life of the believer. James delivers a stinging, brutal indictment of those wealthy members of the church whose faith has failed and who have abused the poor.

The concern for economic justice, the equitable distribution of resources, and the plight of the poor is not tangential to our faith. If Amos has anything to say to us, it is that God will not deal kindly with those who trample the poor. What of those who stand by and allow that to happen?

Jim Holladay

Micah 6:6-8

With what shall I come before the Lord and bow down before the exalted God? Shall I come before him with burnt offerings, with calves a year old? Will the Lord be pleased with thousands of rams, with ten thousand rivers of oil? Shall I offer my firstborn for my transgression, the fruit of my body for the sin of my soul? He has showed you, O man, what is good. And what does the Lord require of you? To act justly and to love mercy and to walk humbly with your God.

As director of a refugee resettlement program, I was expecting a critical phone call from the State Department. During those days, our eight outgoing telephone lines were constantly busy with local and out of the state phone calls. So, I instructed our receptionist to keep line #1 open. "Whatever you do," I said, "please do not use line one. I am expecting a very important phone call from the State Department and it should come within the next 15 minutes." After 30 minutes of agonizing expectation, I checked with the switchboard operator, "Have you kept line #1 clear?" "Yes, sir, I have not moved from here," she responded and added, "in fact, every time a telephone call came in on that line, I quickly picked up the receiver, and then hung up without saying a word in order to make totally sure that the line stayed clear."

Faithfulness to the task when undermined with negligence of the outcome, invalidates the most sincere efforts. Likewise, regardless of frequency and quantity, sacrificial giving and worshipping are nullified when they are disconnected from daily life events. From its creation, the purpose of humanity was to be instrumental in the maintenance of creation. Abraham was called to be a blessing to others. The nation that his offspring produced was to be a blessing to other nations. It is in the daily life events that we validate God's creation as it relates to us and we to God. For Micah, a person walks with God not only within the confines of the sanctuary. Fairness, justice, and mercy toward other human beings, are necessary ingredients in the cycle of the worshipping experience. Without these, any efforts to please God will be in vain.

Donoso S. Escobar

XX
Matthew 11:2-6

> When John heard in prison what Christ was doing, he sent his disciples to ask him, "Are you the one who was to come, or should we expect someone else?" Jesus replied, "Go back and report to John what you hear and see: The blind receive sight, the lame walk, those who have leprosy are cured, the deaf hear, the dead are raised, and the good news is preached to the poor. Blessed is the man who does not fall away on account of me."

As I read this passage I think of social ministry almost immediately. Jesus was concerned not only about the spiritual condition of the people but their physical and emotional needs as well. His style of ministry made many question his Messiahship. In verse 6 he states, "Blessed is the man who does fall away on account of me." It appears that there were some who rejected him because of the kind of ministry he conducted. The blessed were those who accepted him as a servant Messiah rather than a conquering Messiah.

A popular aphorism of our day is "seeing is believing." However, I have embedded that statement in my mind because for some people believing comes only after seeing Christ through another's actions. At the early stage of my call to the ministry the only vocations I knew were pastor or missionary. I learned, however, that ministry often led to other kinds of service. While in college I served as an Assistant Chaplain in a hospital trauma center. It was there I began to realize the significance of "seeing is believing."

As we go about daily work, may we remind ourselves that "faith is not blind." There may be individuals watching our actions to see how we live before trusting the faith we profess.

Ricky Creech

Matthew 15:21-28

Leaving that place, Jesus withdrew to the region of Tyre and Sidon. A Canaanite woman from that vicinity came to him, crying out, "Lord, Son of David, have mercy on me! My daughter is suffering terribly from demon-possession." Jesus did not answer a word. So his disciples came to him and urged him, "Send her away, for she keeps crying out after us." He answered, "I was sent only to the lost sheep of Israel." The woman came and knelt before him. "Lord, help me!" she said. He replied, "It is not right to take the children's bread and toss it to their dogs." "Yes, Lord, she said, "but even the dogs eat the crumbs that fall from their masters' table." Then Jesus answered, "Woman, you have great faith! Your request is granted." And her daughter was healed from that very hour.

The writer of the book of Hebrews stated that "... faith is being sure of what we hope for and certain of what we do not see." The character of this woman described here by Matthew is very clear. She was a Canaanite woman and therefore non-Jewish. Yet in spite of the prejudice she experienced from Jews, she turned to a Jewish rabbi in the hope that he could help her daughter.

She is aware of Jesus' initial mission to the "lost sheep of Israel," but this does not prevent her from proclaiming him "Lord, Son of David." Her daughter is suffering and something inside her convinces her that her non-Jewish status is just not that important. She humbly approaches Jesus yet there is boldness in her desire for assistance. It is this woman's great faith that moves Jesus to action immediately.

Although one might feel as though they are not one of the chosen or preferred group, faith in the Lord Jesus always brings about a positive response from the Lord. In fact, the Hebrew writer later proclaims (11:6), "But without faith, it is impossible to please Him, for he who comes to God must believe that He is, and that He is a rewarder of those who diligently seek Him." This Canaanite woman exhibited great faith. She believed that he was indeed "Lord, Son of David." She was rewarded because she risked diligently seeking the assistance of the Lord.

Social workers, as they engage in very difficult situations, can learn much from the faith that the Canaanite woman exhibited.

T. Vaughn Walker

Matthew 25:31-46

When the Son of Man comes in his glory, and all the angels with him, he will sit on his throne in heavenly glory. All the nations will be gathered before him, and he will separate the people one from another as a shepherd separates the sheep from the goats. He will put the sheep on his right and goats on his left. Then the King will say to those on his right, 'Come, you who are blessed by my Father, take your inheritance, the kingdom prepared for you since the creation of the world. For I was hungry and you gave me something to eat. I was thirsty and you gave me something to drink. I was a stranger and you invited me in. I needed clothes and you clothed me. I was sick and you looked after me, I was in prison and you came to visit me.'

Then the righteous will answer him, 'Lord, when did we see you hungry and feed you, or thirsty and give you something to drink? When did we see you a stranger and invite you in, or needing clothes and clothe you? When did we see you sick or in prison and go to visit you?' The King will reply, 'I tell you the truth, whatever you did for one of the least of these brothers of mine, you did for me.'

Then he will say to those on his left, 'Depart from me, you who are cursed, into the eternal fire prepared for the devil and his angels. For I was hungry and you gave me nothing to eat, I was thirsty and you gave me nothing to drink. I was a stranger and you did not invite me in. I needed clothes and you did not clothe me. I was sick and in prison and you did not look after me.' They also will answer, 'Lord, when did we see you hungry or thirsty or a stranger or needing clothes or sick or in prison, and did not help you?' He will reply, 'I tell you the truth, whatever you did not do for one of the least of these, you did not do for me.' Then they will go away to eternal punishment, but the righteous to eternal life.

Whenever a social worker is asked to speak to a church about social ministries, the scripture for the day is most likely to be from Matthew 25. It may be that when we read this scripture in private devotion, we feel a bit smug. When Jesus comes, we will certainly be among the sheep who will be rewarded. We have given our lives to clothing, visiting, and feeding the needy and to prodding the church to do so. Our time is coming.

One thing should make us uncomfortable, though. As Jesus tells it, the sheep don't know that they are sheep. They are surprised to find that they have been serving the Lord. Where does that leave us? How can we be the sheep if we are expecting to be sheep? Can we somehow slam shut our Bibles, hoping we can reclaim our innocence? We cannot. We are caught in a paradox, knowing that giving cold water brings reward, yet being told that we are to love without figuring up the benefits.

We should remember the goats. Their response to the Son of Man is, "When did we not serve you?" They thought they had done what was required and had earned an A. They had been self consciously religious, looking out for ways to demonstrate their faith. "If we had known it was you, of course, we would have ministered to you, Jesus!" In contrast, the sheep are surprised because they have given spontaneously, not self-consciously. They did it because their hearts had been transformed by the Good Shepherd's love. They did what came naturally.

Somehow we must live in the tension of doing what is expected, but disciplining ourselves so that our doing springs from a transformed spirit. It is not only how I respond to the needy client, but the family member, friend, or hostile church member needing my time, my concern, my giving. Help me, Lord, not to be satisfied with professional caregiving but to seek to allow my whole life and my every relationship to reflect your love and self- giving.

Diana Garland

Mark 7:20-23

> He went on: "What comes out of a man is what makes him 'unclean.' For from within, out of men's hearts, come evil thoughts, sexual immorality, theft, murder, adultery, greed, malice, deceit, lewdness, envy, slander, arrogance and folly. All these evils come from inside and make a man 'unclean.'"

Chapter seven of Mark begins with the Pharisees and some of the scribes gathered around Jesus where some of the disciples ate with unwashed hands. Immediately, the Jews put the question to Jesus: "Why do your disciples not live according to the tradition of the elders, but eat with hands defiled?" Jesus said this situation was like the days of Isaiah when people were more interested in tradition than in worshiping God. Jesus told them that they rejected God's commandments in order to keep their tradition.

This passage reinforces these words. Jesus says that what comes out of the person is what defiles. The emphasis is on the heart of the person. Specific examples are given to explain some of the conditions that come out of a person: evil thoughts, fornication, theft, murder, adultery, coveting, wickedness, deceit, licentiousness, envy, slander, pride, and foolishness. These are the things that defile us; not anything from the outside.

How often have Christians argued and debated over tradition. The frequently used words are: "We haven't done it that way before." Sometimes, people seem to be saying, "We don't care what the Bible says, we do it this way."

Memories and history can be helpful and healthy but not when they become an obstruction to God. In this passage, Jesus warns us to be aware of our values, motivations, and behaviors; these are the things that defile us.

Pat Bailey

Mark 10:13-16

People were bringing little children to Jesus to have him touch them, but the disciples rebuked them. When Jesus saw this, he was indignant. He said to them, "Let the little children come to me, and do not hinder them, for the kingdom of God belongs to such as these. I tell you the truth, anyone who will not receive the kingdom of God like a little child will never enter it." And he took the children in his arms, put his hands on them and blessed them.

Jesus' saying about children must have come as a shock to those who heard him; in his world, children were second-class citizens. Although they might grow up to be productive and protective of their parents, until then, they stood far down the social ladder—behind even women, the poor, the sick, and the lame. Paul said, "When I was a child, I thought like a child. But when I became a man, I put away childish things"—hardly a glorification of childhood! Neither did Jesus idealize childhood. Instead, He was saying, "In my kingdom, the very last, even helpless, valueless, dependent children, those who count for nothing in this world, shall come first."

I don't find it difficult to love children, to want to touch their hair and soak in the grins and laughter. I like to watch a school-age child's excitement over new ideas grasped for the first time. Unlike Jesus' world, our society romanticizes children; we use our affection for children to sell everything from long distance phone companies to Campbell's soup.

It is the harder thing, though, to look beyond the lovable children that touch us to the systems that hurt children. It is hard to figure out the complexity of issues that insidiously destroy families who, though they may not be like us middle class folks, are, nevertheless, the very best place for their children to live and grow. I think Jesus calls us to do the harder thing, though. He not only took children in his arms, but he attacked the systems of his society that burdened people to the point that they could not care for one another, as in his attack on their tithing as an excuse for not caring for their own aging parents. Jesus put people before systems, and he put children at the very front of the line. In their helplessness and their dependence, they model how to relate to God for those of us who think we are powerful and wise. "Those who are last shall be first." And Jesus calls us not only to relate to God as children, but to follow his example in blessing the children of this world.

Diana Garland

Mark 14:27-31

"You will all fall away," Jesus told them, "for it is written: 'I will strike the shepherd, and the sheep will be scattered,' But after I have risen, I will go ahead of you into Galilee." Peter declared, "Even if all fall away, I will not." "I tell you the truth," Jesus answered, "today—yes, tonight—before the rooster crows twice you yourself will disown me three times." But Peter insisted emphatically, "Even if I have to die with you, I will never disown you." And all the others said the same.

Often I have to have a heart to heart talk with my tongue. The focus of these conversations usually is the quick promise or resolution which seems to jump from my mouth of its own volition. Some tasks need to be done or some commitment needs to be made and there is silence in the group. Up jumps my mouth to "do its thing."

Peter must have suffered from this same problem. For when Jesus said that all the disciples would fall away, Peter was quick to say that "though all may fall away, yet I will not." Peter's tongue had done its thing.

Jesus, however, knew things that Peter did not know about the cost of keeping resolutions and promises. Jesus knew human nature. He knew that talk is cheap and action is costly. Jesus knew that when survival was in question Peter would deny him.

Perhaps nothing is more important in helping people than being careful to make only those promises and resolutions we can keep. Many people who come to us for help do so because they have been the victims of "jobs of the tongue."

I can hear my dad saying, "If you say you are going to do it, then do it. Your word is your bond. If you aren't going to do it, keep your mouth shut." Well Dad, it is easier said than done!

Thank God there was forgiveness for Peter and there is forgiveness for me!

Anne Davis

Luke 4:18-21

The Spirit of the Lord is on me, because he has anointed me to preach good news to the poor. He has sent me to claim freedom for the prisoners and recovery of sight for the blind, to release the oppressed, to proclaim the year of the Lord's favor." Then he rolled up the scroll, gave it back to the attendant and sat down. The eyes of everyone in the synagogue were fastened on him, and he began by saying to them, "Today this scripture is fulfilled in your hearing."

Jesus had just returned from the temptation in the wilderness to minister in Galilee. In the synagogue in Nazareth, Jesus claimed that he fulfilled the prophecy from Isaiah 61:1-2. The people responded in amazement that this carpenter's son would make such a declaration.

They missed the point. Jesus was not "just" anointed; he was anointed for a purpose—to bring good news, freedom, sight, release! Jesus was sent to the poor, the prisoner, the blind, the oppressed! If they could not accept Jesus as fulfillment of prophecy, how much less could they accept his mission to the outcasts.

They needed the message Jesus brought. They were unable to keep every letter of the law, yet they would not hear the good news of the New Testament. They were prisoners of their own narrow understandings, yet they would not let Jesus unlock the prison gate. They were blind to the Messiah standing before them, and they would not accept Jesus' healing touch.

Lyle Greene

XXVII
Luke 19:1-10

Jesus entered Jericho and was passing through. A man was there by the name of Zacchaeus; he was a chief tax collector and was wealthy. He wanted to see who Jesus was, but being a short man he could not, because of the crowd. So he ran ahead and climbed a sycamore-fig tree to see him, since Jesus was coming that way. When Jesus reached the spot, he looked up and said to him, "Zacchaeus, come down immediately. I must stay at your house today." So he came down at once and welcomed him gladly. All the people saw this and began to mutter, "He has gone to be the guest of a 'sinner.'" But Zacchaeus stood up and said to the Lord, "Look, Lord! Here and now I give half of my possessions to the poor, and if I have cheated anybody out of anything, I will pay back four times the amount." Jesus said to him, "Today salvation has come to this house, because this man, too, is a son of Abraham. For the Son of Man came to seek and to save what was lost."

Social workers know what it means to minister with people who ask us for help, who are oppressed and hurting. In the previous passage, Luke 18:35-43, Jesus approaches the gates of Jericho and heals the blind man sitting by the roadside calling—"Jesus, Son of David, have mercy on me!" Just as Jesus heard his cries, we hear echoing in our minds the cries of our own clients for healing for the hurts life has brought them. Much of our energy and professional commitment goes toward finding the resources, developing the skills, and opening ourselves to God's power so that we in turn can be instruments of Good News to those who call out.

But what about Zacchaeus? He is neither blind nor lame; he is not even asking how to inherit eternal life. He is only curious, watching safely from a distance, high in a tree. How does a social worker respond to such people? Too often, I am afraid, we see wealthy people as resources to be claimed for our clients—funding resources, or perhaps volunteers. We strongly proclaim the dignity and worth of every person, yet somehow, people like Zacchaeus seem to have more than their share of both dignity and worth.

We can learn from Jesus' relationship with Zacchaeus. As aloof (or at least aloft!) and wealthy as Zacchaeus may have been, Jesus could see that he was isolated, cut off from his own community. And so Jesus addressed his need: "Zacchaeus, come down immediately. I must stay at your house today." He challenged Zacchaeus to "get involved," but the challenge to service was one which at the same time responded to the deepest need of Zacchaeus. Jesus truly cared for Zacchaeus the man, not Zacchaeus the funding source, or Zacchaeus the potential volunteer. We do not know what they talked about at Zacchaeus' house, but the results are a social worker's fantasy: Zacchaeus gave generously to the poor.

Seeking and saving the lost requires caring enough to see the reality and worth of every person as God's child.

Diana Garland

XXVIII
John 1:14

The Word became flesh and made his dwelling among us.
We have seen his glory, the glory of the One and Only, who
came from the Father, full of grace and truth.

I do not claim to be a big expert about gardening. Since I live in an
apartment, watching "The Victory Garden" on PBS is about as close as I
get to growing fruits and vegetables. When it comes to apples, I know
some types are good for eating and others are better for cooking and
baking, but I don't know which is which. Most of my personal experience with apples comes from eating them covered with peanut butter.
It's nice to combine the juiciness of the fruit with the creamy-crunchy
texture of the peanut butter. Eventually, I run out of apple, and all that I
have left is the core. In my opinion, the best part of the apple is gone,
But from the apple's point of view, the core is the most important part.
The core contains the seeds—the life-giving, regenerational portion of
the apple. Because of the core and its seeds, the life cycle of the apple
can continue and bear more fruit.

When people saw Jesus' life and ministry, some did not see the real
value of Jesus' work. He was viewed as just another prophet who would
pass from the scene. Others were able to see the core of the matter revealed in Jesus' miracles and teachings. Since both groups were looking
at the same person, the difference must have depended on their expec-
tations. When we encounter individuals, how do we see them? As we
deal with clients and parishioners, how do we locate the seeds of life in
them? At first glance, it may appear that all good has been taken from
their lives by oppressive systems. We have heard their stories a hundred
times before.

Can we see the intrinsic value and imago dei of every person? Instead
of focusing on the brokenness, I hope that our ministries can help people
see their own potential and worth. May God guide us to nurture the
seeds of hope in the people we meet!

Alice Tennis

John 12:1-8

Six days before the Passover, Jesus arrived at Bethany, where Lazarus lived, whom Jesus had raised from the dead. Here a dinner was given in Jesus' honor. Martha served, while Lazarus was among those reclining at the table with him. Then Mary took about a pint of pure nard, an expensive perfume; she poured it on Jesus' feet and wiped his feet with her hair. And the house was filled with the fragrance of the perfume. But one of his disciples, Judas Iscariot, who was later to betray him, objected, "Why wasn't this perfume sold and the money given to the poor? It was worth a year's wages." He did not say this because he cared about the poor but because he was a thief; as keeper of the money bag, he used to help himself to what was put into it. "Leave her alone," Jesus replied. "It was intended that she should save this perfume for the day of my burial. You will always have the poor among you, but you will not always have me."

Few statements in the Bible have been taken out of context more than "the poor always ye have with you." I have heard it often used as an excuse to keep from taking the needs of the poor seriously. Such an interpretation is in direct contrast to many examples in the scripture which depict Jesus tenderly, and with great sensitivity, ministering to t
he needs of the poor.

In context, Jesus was calling His disciples in this passage to keep their priorities in proper order. Mary had poured expensive perfume on His feet and Judas Iscariot had objected with the question, "Why wasn't this perfume sold and the money given to the poor?" Jesus' response was that even the needs of the poor would have to take a second place to the preparation for His burial. He was saying, "First things first."

What a word for those of us who spend our time ministering to the poor. Could it be that we too could get so involved in what we are doing that we forget to put our attention on Christ first? Could it be that the needs of people are so great and the demands on our time so numerous that we forget to take time to attend to our own spiritual growth and devotions?

It may well be that we can only truly minister to the poor in Jesus' name if we have taken time to put Him first in our lives and let our ministry come out of the overflow.

Anne Davis

Acts 2:46-47

Every day they continued to meet together in the temple courts. They broke bread in their homes and ate together with glad and sincere hearts, praising God and enjoying the favor of all the people. And the Lord added to their number daily those who were being saved.

What a party! The believers had come together for fellowship, to enjoy one another's company and praise God. God was doing a great work among the people and they could not help but celebrate. What better reason is there to have a party?

Growing up in a large family I was able to experience a lot of celebrations. We not only celebrated numerous birthdays, graduations, and weddings, we also made up things just so we could have a party. Such celebrations included job promotions, the birth of a new calf, moving the wood pile, and having a freshly mowed lawn. One of our favorite forms of celebration involved dragging out the old family slide show. Even though these slides were watched twice a year, we enjoyed them as if we had never seen them before.

Just as my family celebrates a wide variety of events I am also able to celebrate being a part of the family of God. Sometimes we get so caught up in the day to day things of life that we forget to celebrate our calling of reaching out to others. God often uses us to touch the hearts of the hurting which can bring about healing and change. We are called to a life of proclaiming God's love both through word and deed. I am sweetly reminded of the old hymn, "Redeemed, how I love to proclaim it."

May God continue to use us as instruments in adding to the Kingdom and grant us strength and wisdom as we celebrate and carry out the ministry to which God has called us.

Von Hulin

Acts 7:59-8:1

While they were stoning him, Stephen prayed, "Lord Jesus, receive my spirit." Then he fell on his knees and cried out, "Lord, do not hold this sin against them." When he had said this, he fell asleep. And Saul was there, giving approval to his death. On that day a great persecution broke out against the church at Jerusalem, and all except the apostles were scattered throughout Judea and Samaria.

Luke, the writer of the Book of Acts, in his introduction of Stephen in Chapter six, verse five, describes him as "a man full of faith and of the Holy Spirit." Later in verse eight of the same chapter, Stephen is described as one full of faith and power who did great wonders and miracles among the people.

Faith and the active presence of the Spirit of God in one's life is essential in becoming the powerful witness God wants to use for his glory. Although many in the synagogue disputed with Stephen, Luke tells us that they were not able to resist the wisdom and the spirit by which he spoke. Even though they set up false witnesses against him, Stephen didn't let that prevent him from being the powerful witness needed for his time. Stephen spoke boldly and courageously against much opposition and hostility. Because he was one full of the Holy Spirit, Stephen remained steadfast.

As Saul observed Stephen crying out to the Lord as they stoned him, "Lord, lay not this sin to their charge," we need to be reminded that there are those watching us go through our trials and tribulations. The question remains, are we the powerful witness needed for our day? We can be a powerful witness if we would seek continually a fresh filling of God's Spirit in our lives regardless of the situation in which we are confronted.

T. Vaughn Walker

Romans 6:1-4

What shall we say, then? Shall we go on sinning so that grace may increase? By no means! We died to sin; how can we live in it any longer? Or don't you know that all of us who were baptized into Christ Jesus were baptized into his death? We were therefore buried with him through baptism into death in order that, just as Christ was raised from the dead through the glory of the Father, we too may live a new life.

"Shall we persist in sin so that there may be all the more grace?" Paul knew that his position on this question was being misunderstood and distorted. This question refers to his doctrine of justification by faith and his teachings about living under law. Some were interpreting his teachings to mean that sin is acceptable behavior for Christians; a Christian is not obliged to live morally and ethically, and perhaps has good reason to sin. "The more you sin the more grace your receive."

This notion, of course, is wholly illogical. If we persist in sin, we create a world that is out of step with God's kingdom. Sin rules by death and sin rewards with death. How, then, can sin bring profit to anyone who has entered a new life in Christ?

Paul emphatically rejects this twisted notion that sin is acceptable and profitable. How, he inquired, could a Christian manage to continue living in sin? We are dead to sin. We are in union with Christ. We have been re-created in God's image. His image is the core and essence of our new being and new life. Where then could be found within our being the stuff that such sinfulness would require?

In fact, Paul asserts, it is impossible to "persist in sin" and at the same time to "set our feet upon the new path of life." God calls us to live out of and up to His image. Our new life requires obedience to God's purpose—like Christ—a lifestyle that abounds in service. Where would we find the time or energy to persist in sin? Those of us who love the Lord and are called according to His purpose are busy living His Word—loving kindness, challenging oppression, showing mercy, and doing justice.

We have no reason to worry about increasing or earning God's grace. He has sufficient grace and He grants it freely. That "Grace rules by means of righteousness, leading us to eternal life through Jesus Christ our Lord." We will "profit" if we simply accept the gift of His Son, live under the rule of His measureless grace, and daily walk the path of the new life.

Sandra Hill

I Corinthians 13:4-8a

Love is patient and kind; love is not jealous or boastful; it is not arrogant or rude. Love does not insist on its own way; it is not irritable or resentful; it does not rejoice at wrong, but rejoices in the right. Love bears all things, believes all things, hopes all things, endures all things. Love never ends.

This famous passage about love is often read as an exhortation to practice love. It is, however, much more than that. It is an analysis of a relationship that is essential to social work and can perhaps best be expressed in the word 'concern'. Concern is a mindset that transcends the rather facile and indeed selfish emotions of 'liking' and 'disliking'.

I once had a student in administration who took as her project learning how to supervise a worker whom she thoroughly disliked, justifiably, as far as I could see. At first she tried very hard to like this woman but that only made my student guilty and quite unable to hold her to good performance. She was not able to do her job until she came into my office one day, banged her fist on my desk, and said, "I hate that woman, but I do care what happens to her."

The command to love one's enemies does not mean that we must make them into friends, although it is pleasant when that can be done. The command is to care what happens to our enemies while they are still hostile to us and maybe to everything we care about.

Alan Keith-Lucas

XXXIV
I Corinthinians 15:58

Therefore, my dear brothers, stand firm. Let nothing move you. Always give yourselves fully to the work of the Lord, because you know that your labor in the Lord is not in vain.

Several years ago, I heard Joyce Hollyday, co-editor of "Sojourners" magazine, talk about her then recent trip to South Africa. She told the story of a young man named Tommy who accompanied her and her husband as they walked through the streets of Soweto. At one point, the three of them were suddenly surrounded by government police, complete with rifles and a tank. At gunpoint they were taken for questioning. Joyce did not greatly fear for herself or her husband, as she knew that the government would be hesitant to do any real harm to American citizens. But she did fear greatly for Tommy, who had just been released from prison after a ten-month stay during which time he was tortured repeatedly.

After questioning Joyce and her husband, the interrogator turned to Tommy and began to abuse him verbally, threatening to detain him and calling him "no good." Tommy responded by reaching into his breast pocket and pulling out a copy of the New Testament. Holding it up in front of the interrogator's face, he declared, "I am a Christian." A silence fell upon the room as Tommy stood firm before the face of evil and injustice.

The Apostle Paul reminds us to be "Steadfast, immovable, always abounding in the work of the Lord." And though you and I are seldom, if ever, confronted with the deep, dark, pervasive kind of injustice that Tommy and his friends are confronted with each day, we too, have opportunity to stand firm daily in the face of evil and injustice. We too, have a charge to keep. May God grant us the grace to keep the charge that God has given us to remain steadfast and immovable in the face of injustice. We know deep in our hearts that life is more than flesh and blood and that the work we do in the name of Christ is never in vain.

Cindy Weber

Ephesians 4:1-6

As a prisoner for the Lord, then, I urge you to live a life worthy of the calling you have received. Be completely humble and gentle; be patient, bearing with one another in love. Make every effort to keep the unity of the Spirit through the bond of peace. There is one body and one Spirit—just as you were called to one hope when you were called—one Lord, one faith, one baptism; one God and Father of all, who is over all and through all and in all.

"Why do I work in the church? Is it worth it?" Paul must have asked these questions. He spent his whole converted life establishing groups of people who bickered and backslid. He gave of himself and they questioned his motives. Surely Paul had doubts.

But Paul's doubts led to renewed commitment. The first three chapters of Ephesians paint one of the most beautiful portraits of the church found in scripture. It's a description of a people being knit together and filled with God. It's the church we long for.

And Paul does not end his epistle in the heavens. He returns to the place where you and I actually experience the church. After offering us a vision of incomparable glory, he tells us to continue doing the mundane, everyday tasks of the Christian life: enduring one another, being patient, trying to hold things together.

Paul demonstrates that there is nothing quite so practical as good theory. For when we can envision unity then we can "make every effort to keep the unity." When we can picture peace, then we can "be humble and gentle." When we understand God's hope for the church and the world, then we can set about seeking wholeness and well-being.

Kay Whitten

XXXVI
Philippians 2:1-5

If you have any encouragement from being united with Christ, if any comfort from his love, if any fellowship with the Spirit, if any tenderness and compassion, then make my joy complete by being like-minded, have the same love, being one in spirit and purpose. Do nothing out of selfish ambition or vain conceit, but in humility consider others better than yourselves. Each of you should look not only to your own interests, but also to the interests of others. Your attitude should be the same as that of Christ Jesus.

Being a social worker is not an easy life. It requires a great deal of dedication and personal sacrifice. Unfortunately, the sacrifices more often than not result in physical, emotional, and spiritual stress. This stress usually leads us to adopt a position of self-preservation, that is, we have time or make time only for ourselves and/or our families.

Given these circumstances how then do we go about doing more than merely surviving our work? I would suggest we follow Paul's recommendation in Philippians and look after one another. He calls for us to be "of one mind." Such action will require us to set aside competitiveness and selfishness as we show an increased concern for the well being of one another. We need to lift one another up through support and encouragement of a tangible nature, not just a pat on the back and a few well chosen words. This will mean having to make time for colleagues. That, however, is what servanthood and friendship are all about. Paul urges us on to such behavior; Jesus has called for us to "love our neighbors as ourselves." Such empowerment is the essence of social work.

David M. Ramsey

XXXVII
Colossians 1:27

To them God has chosen to make known among the Gentiles the glorious riches of this mystery, which is Christ in you, the hope of glory.

Hope in the New Testament does not suggest desire. It has nothing to do with wishing on a star or wishing on anything else. Christian hope is expectation. Expectation of what? Expectation that the promises of God will be fulfilled.

What could a person in prison know about hope? Is it not ironic that the one in prison, Paul, writes to those who are physically free about hope? Paul felt free in prison because he was confident that God would complete what God had begun in him (Phil. 1:6). The Colossians on the other hand were being bound by false teachings about Christ and were beginning to surrender their freedom in Christ.

Social workers must not confuse "hope" with "desire." There is hope that we can overcome every thing and thought that would bind us. There is no human problem that cannot be overcome by our hope. Our hope has a name in a person, "Christ in you, the hope of glory." We must not shift to any false hope. Accept no counterfeit. Don't underestimate the genuine article. Jesus is the hope in whom we can always depend.

Raymond Bailey

I Thessalonians 4:11-12

Make it your ambition to lead a quiet life, to mind your own business and to work with your hands, just as we told you, so that your daily life may win the respect of outsiders and so that you will not be dependent on anybody.

When I first read this verse, I have to admit that I was not very excited. It is not a very social workish verse. "Make it your ambition to lead a quiet life?" Why, I'd rather change the world, make a stir, overthrow some money-changers tables...

But when I'm honest, I realize that most of my days are rather quiet, that most of the things that I do are rather commonplace. There are those days when I feel like I've really done something mighty for the Kingdom. I've really touched a life or made a change. But most of my days, and probably your days too, are spent in doing quiet, ordinary kinds of things.

And so, when I read the Bible, I am greatly encouraged to find that God seems to be primarily revealed to people as they go about their ordinary, everyday lives. Look at Moses, he's tending sheep of all things. Tending sheep is a quiet, ordinary kind of job if there ever was one, and all of a sudden he realizes that he is standing on holy ground. Look at Abraham, he's sitting out on the front porch, resting in the heat of the day, and all of a sudden, these two angels of the Lord appear to him. Look at the two disciples on the Emmaus road. They're just walking along, and all of a sudden, Jesus walks with them.

God is present in the midst of our quiet, everyday lives. And everything that we do, no matter how quiet or simple or commonplace, everything that we do, if done to please God, is holy. So take off your shoes this day. You too are on holy ground.

Cindy Weber

II Timothy 2:15

Do your best to present yourself to God as one approved, a workman who does not need to be ashamed and who correctly handles the word of truth.

When helping others gets especially difficult, the most difficult advice to follow is "endure." Yet this second letter from a veteran missionary to a younger missionary urges endurance as a major quality for any minister, young or old. This is not a stoic "grin and bear it" but rather a "tolerate, look and grow." Handling aright the Word of Truth means hanging on long enough to experience the Word of Truth in the depths.

Handling aright translates a metaphor meaning "to cut straight." We are encouraged to steer life straight rather than veer off course because of stresses, distractions and temptations. If the Word of Truth is our compass then how do we handle it aright? How do we do our best?

The King James Version uses the word "study." It fits the concept of disciple, a learner. We learn from books, from life, from others. In whatever difficulty we may ask, "what does this event have to teach me?" Part of enduring is being teachable. To steer life straight we must learn about ourselves, others and the Word of Truth.

Always we must keep in mind the One for whom we live. Our audience is God. Ask in the difficult times: Who is my audience? Whose approval do I seek? Whose applause ultimately matters?"

Jim England

James 1:27

Religion that God our Father accepts as pure and faultless
is this: to look after orphans and widows in their distress and
to keep oneself from being polluted by the world.

In scriptural times, orphans and widows were powerless and vulnerable people. Here, James indicates that assuming responsibility for these people is one of two evidences that we have pure and undefiled religion. The second evidence is that we keep ourselves unstained by the world.

James gives a clear indication here that pure religion involves both an outward demonstration and an inward discipline. The linking of these two requires a balance between the attention we give to helping others and the attention we give to developing personal righteousness in Christ.

It would seem that our human nature attracts us to "either/or" situations. Some of us want only to work to develop personal righteousness. Neither of these alone is an option according to James. Pure religion links them.

James 1:27 is of great significance to church social workers. The two issues in James are intentionally linked in our very name. Lord, help us to keep in balance our concern for the powerless and vulnerable and our attention to the discipline of personal righteousness! We really do want our religion to be pure and undefiled before you!

Anne Davis

I John 4:7-8

Dear friends, let us love one another, for love comes from God. Everyone who loves has been born of God and knows God. Whoever does not love does not know God, because God is love.

John tells us that "God is love." God loves out of God's very character, but have we so generalized the love of God that it has become another cliche of our culture? We can rob this verse of its profound power by writing it in calligraphy bordered by flowers to be sold in candle shops. We make that love look good, smell sweet and sound so harmless. Such a love will never bother us, but it also will never comfort us. When we generalize the love of God we make it as bland as a warm glass of milk.

We often believe that if God is love God should have power over pain. However, God's love is revealed in pain. As Marjorie Suchocki has written, "the incredible reality revealed on the cross is that God's love does not cease in pain, not even the pain of death. We easily assert that God continues to love us in our pain but what the theology of the cross requires us to acknowledge is that God continues to love in God's pain."

God's love is not vague. It is specific like a person or a cross. God's love is tenacious as well as tender. It is a love that will not let us go. God's love is a suffering love. Elie Wiesel, a survivor of Aushwitz, related in his book Night:

> The S. S. hung two Jewish men and a boy before the assembled inhabitants of the camp. The men died quickly but the death struggle of the boy lasted half an hour. "Where is God? Where is he?", a man behind me asked. As the boy, after a long time, was still in agony on the rope, I heard the man cry again, "Where is God now?" And I heard a voice within me answer, Here he is, he is hanging here on the gallows…"

John writes, "let us love one another; for love is of God."

The love of God is revealed in God's ability to be vulnerable, and suffer with us. We love one another by being vulnerable to each other. We know and express the love of God when we suffer with our sisters and brothers in South Africa, Beijing, or North America. This suffering love for others is not passive or powerless in the face of injustice. It is more than just our emotional response to someone else's pain. This love has the power to make us one with humankind.

Phil Christopher

Revelation 21:3-5

And I heard a loud voice from the throne saying, "Now the dwelling of God is with men, and he will live with them. They will be his people, and God himself will be with them and be their God. He will wipe every tear from their eyes. There will be no more death or mourning or crying or pain, for the old order of things has passed away." He who was seated on the throne said, "I am making everything new."

The book of Revelation has been a source of much controversy among Christians but it need not be. Just as it was written to encourage first century Christians who were facing difficult times, it can be a book that encourages social workers who find themselves exposed daily to the troubles of modern life. The point of Revelation is that we have reason to hope in spite of the overwhelming presence of turmoil in the present. In the midst of tears, mourning, pain, and death, we hold fast to the knowledge that the creation which was made so wonderfully will be restored. We are assured that a time is coming when God will dwell among us and all things will be made new.

Karl Marx believed that such hope led people to ignore the need for change in the present. This may be the outcome for some but many social workers know that such a vision can provide the stamina necessary to continue working for change. The tears of hurting families, the pain of death to loved ones, the repulsiveness of evil deeds which we see daily, these become a heavy burden. A vision of goodness helps lift the weight.

Revelation reminds us that evil is not right. It reminds us that justice, health, life, will be victorious. God Almighty, the inventor of creation with all its majesty, will come to live with us again and will make everything new. The beauty of life will again be as it was intended to be. Though looking to the future unfortunately leads some to ignore the present, it can also help keep the tears, the pain, the mourning, and death in perspective.

Lawrence Ressler